ROBERT CAPA

GROSSMAN PUBLISHERS, INC.
NEW YORK, 1964

IMAGES OF WAR

ROBERT CAPA

with text from his own writings

FOR JULIA

FIRST PRINTING

Designed by Charlotte Trowbridge Dyer

Books by ROBERT CAPA:

Images of War
Report on Israel
      with Irwin Shaw
A Russian Journal
      with John Steinbeck
Slightly out of Focus
The Battle of Waterloo Road
      with Diana Forbes-Robertson
Death in the Making

Acknowledgments:

This book is dedicated to the ideals of photo-journalism, which in turn led to the founding of MAGNUM in 1946, by Robert Capa and his friends, David Seymour, Henri Cartier-Bresson and George Rodger.

Material by Diana Forbes-Robertson from *The Battle of Waterloo Road*, copyright 1941 by Random House, Inc., appears on page 64 with the permission of Random House. The paragraph by Irwin Shaw from *Report on Israel*, copyright 1950 by Simon and Schuster, Inc., appears on page 156 with the permission of Simon and Schuster.

Thanks go to the editiors of *Life* for permission to reprint the story by John Mecklin about Capa's death in Indo-China. Also, many of the photographs in this book were first published in *Life* magazine.

Special thanks are due to John Steinbeck and to *Popular Photography* for permission to use Mr. Steinbeck's article from the magazine.

Printed and bound by Amilcare Pizzi, Milan, Italy.
Produced in collaboration with Chanticleer Press, Inc., New York.

Contents

Photograph by RUTH ORKIN

ROBERT CAPA

An appreciation by JOHN STEINBECK

I know nothing about photography. What I have to say about Capa's is strictly from the point of view of a layman, and the specialists must bear with me. It does seem to me that Capa has proved beyond all doubt that the camera need not be a cold mechanical device. Like the pen, it is as good as the man who uses it. It can be the extension of mind and heart.

Capa's pictures were made in his brain— the camera only completed them. You can no more mistake his work than you can the canvas of a fine painter. Capa knew what to look for and what to do with it when he found it. He knew, for example, that you cannot photograph war because it is largely an emotion. But he did photograph that emotion by shooting beside it. He could show the horror of a whole people in the face of a child. His camera caught and held emotion.

Capa's work is itself the picture of a great heart and an overwhelming compassion. No one can take his place. No one can take the place of any fine artist, but we are fortunate to have in his pictures the quality of the man.

I worked and traveled with Capa a great deal. He may have had closer friends but he had none who loved him more. It was his pleasure to seem casual and careless about his work. He was not. His pictures are not accidents. The emotion in them did not come by chance. He could photograph motion and gaiety and heartbreak. He could photograph thought. He made a world and it was Capa's world.

The greatness of Capa is twofold. We have his pictures, a true and vital record of our time—ugly and beautiful, set down by the mind of an artist. But Capa had another work which may be even more important. He gathered young men about him, encouraged, instructed, even fed and clothed them; but, best, he taught them respect for their art and integrity in its performance. He proved to them that a man can live by this medium and still be true to himself. And never once did he try to get them to take his kind of picture. Thus the effect of Capa will be found in the men who worked with him. They will carry a little part of Capa all their lives and perhaps hand him on to their young men.

It is very hard to think of being without Capa. I don't think I have accepted that fact yet. But I suppose we should be thankful that there is so much of him with us still.

7

At the opening of each section of this book, a short paragraph sets the time and the place of Capa's involvement in what follows. The writing that appears with the photographs themselves is Robert Capa's own writing, from his published books, from his notes, and from his letters.

Robert Capa found truth in war; he loathed it, but he understood it and stayed close to the front lines. He had lived under the tyranny of Horthy in Hungary and knew intimately the kind of oppression that breeds war. He went to an actual battlefront for the first time in Spain in 1936. In the course of eighteen years, he photographed five wars.

Capa was forty-one years old in 1954, when he was killed by a land mine at Thai Binh, North Vietnam, while taking pictures of French combat troops. The French awarded him a Croix de Guerre with the palm, order of the Army, one of France's highest honors.

Seeds of War

Robert Capa first took up his camera in the early thirties, and whether or not he was aware of it, the conflicts and tensions of Europe in that decade formed the pattern of his future as a photographer and journalist. His love of people, his quick understanding and sympathy for the suffering of the individual, made it impossible for him to ignore the political events which were affecting the lives of everyone he saw. Capa began then to record political emotions and the emergence of unalterably opposed political faiths. In the center of the conflict stood Capa's real protagonist: the little man whose future was at stake in a world he could not change. Again and again this protagonist appears in the pictures on the pages of this book. The pictures are accompanied by quotations from Capa's own writings—books, letters, articles—and, in a few cases, from the writing other people did to appear with Capa's photographs.

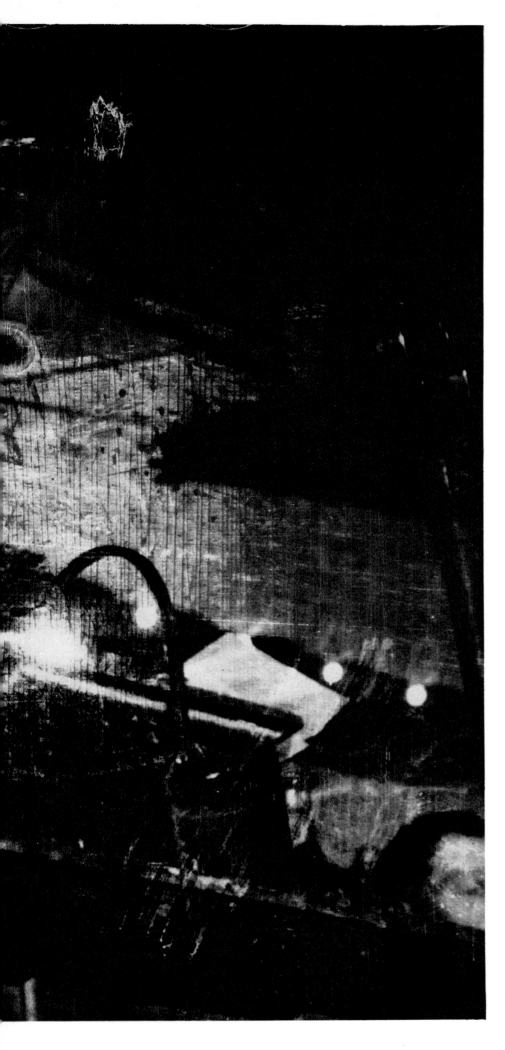

Robert Capa's first published photograph.
Leon Trotsky, Copenhagen, 1931

World War I veterans, Paris, 1936

I talked with a distraught Italian militiaman
on the line of the Franco-Italian frontier
in a second-class compartment which
we occupied alone. The green-uniformed
good-looking young man soon became very
daring and began to chat when he saw
that nobody could hear us. He attacked
the big newspaper headlines which shouted
about German pogroms, British armaments
and Spanish civil war:

"It is a terrible disappoint-
ment we met. At the beginning of October
we believed that war and hunger are
finished. And now we see that everything
is on the old: we have as uneatable bread
as before and we are going to face the
same danger of massacre and useless death
as in the passed thrillful months . . . No
one of us knows exactly what's going on
in the world and in our country but many
signs show that all—our revolution before
18 years, Ethiopia, Spain, our alliance with
the worst enemy, Hitler—all these were
in vain and our life won't turn to be
better . . . Perhaps war could help us, if
we should march with France and Great
Britain against Germany. But war . . . It
is terrible . . ."

"What brings on this horror
of war?" I asked him. "Many of your
men are joining Franco with enthusiasm
in the Spanish Civil War." He became
indignant:

Verdun, 1937

14

German veterans honor their countrymen dead
in World War I, Verdun, 1937

Seeds of War   French Communists, Paris, 1936

Paris, 1936

"Without the intention of a political dispute, dear sir, listen to the followings. I am 38 years old and I am a soldier because nobody could give me any work since years. My father is a little merchant almost as poor as a beggar. I have four sisters and brothers standing day by day before starving. And in Spain: Italian 'volunteers' receive monthly 600 lire as common soldiers and 3,000 lire as officers. We had no expenses at the front and so we can send to home this whole sum saving ours from starving. I did the same until I did not loose my left arm. Now here I am, a nobody wearing a uniform. It was not a good business, you can believe me . . ."

Seeds of War

Bastille Day, Paris, 1937

Spain

In 1936, Capa went to Spain to report on the war there. From then on, his own special gifts and the course of world events led him into the role of a professional photographer of wars. In Spain he recorded for the first time the kind of scenes that he was later to see repeated again and again. In Spain, he took his classic picture of man and war—the Spanish Loyalist at the instant of death. Gerda Taro, a photojournalist whom Capa had fallen in love with in Paris, went with him to the Spanish front. Together they worked a year covering the war. They produced a book called **Death in the Making,** but Gerda never saw it. She was crushed to death by a tank in the confusion of a retreat. The dedication page (opposite) was Capa's tribute to her.

FOR GERDA TARO,

WHO SPENT ONE YEAR AT THE SPANISH FRONT,

AND WHO STAYED ON.

Madrid, December, 1937.   R.C.

Sometimes the shelling lags; the enemy rests on his haunches; and on such mornings the defenders of Madrid take the sun, read, play chess, write letters home which, when they arrive, will be no guarantee that the sender is still alive. The war has become routine; the abnormal, as always, has become normal. In their dugouts the soldiers do not feel as men feel in dugouts on far fronts. The dugouts are the outposts of their homes; this is their home.

The new army is an army of youth. And they enlist voluntarily. The issue is clear. It is their fight to defend their homes, their culture, their very lives against a general who cannot govern while they live.

They grew up together in the villages, worked side by side in the shops, the laboratories, and now fight side by side to hold what they won.

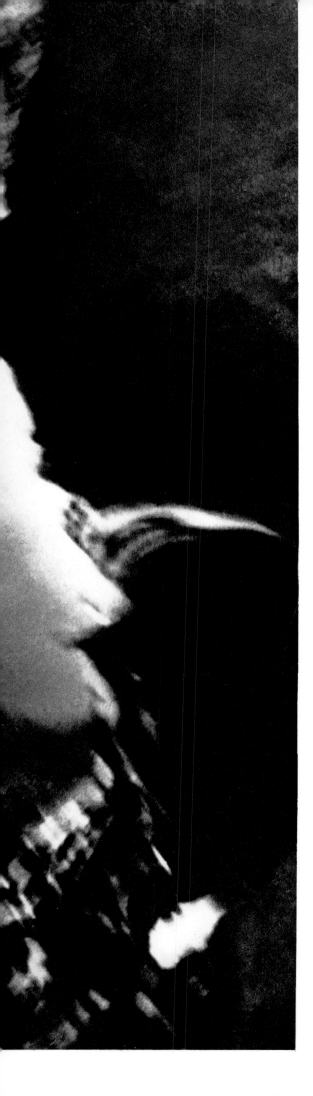

The attack is about to begin. The division's motto is "Spare Nothing." In a few minutes the officers arrange last-minute details and the commissar still finds time to make a quick speech to the battalion. His words are full of passion, but his voice is calm and firm. His *"Venga, venga"* (forward) will remain in everybody's ears, no matter what happens. Now the men start walking forward, in single file. They spread out in almost a semi-circle around the hills. So far their march is protected by the folds of the terrain. Around them, reserve sectors stand waiting. After a curve in the road the climb begins, and from this moment on the men are no longer covered. The enemy is higher up, above the assailants' heads. The noise of their projectiles begins to fill the air. This is the critical moment. Men detach themselves and go forward by leaps and bounds, doubled over. The movement takes on speed. The men in the back must keep running if they don't want to lose the ones in front. In this kind of war there are no longer trenches but only a few protected spots like squares on a chessboard. One by one the men run toward the next firing zone.

The enemy concentrates his artillery at the top of the hills; twenty grenades per minute. The "Marineros" throw themselves into holes in the ground and hollows in the cliffs. Despite the fire they do not stop picking up their wounded. Many of them need medical aid, including some enemy wounded.

At the end of this day of battle the artillery fire still does not slow down. In spite of this, the men have started to eat. The first reports come in: four lines of different heights have been captured, all the orders of the day have been carried out, the bridgehead is blocked. The next task will be even more difficult: maintaining the new positions.

Above the stream of refugees fly enemy planes, and on the road there is no defense against them. Those on the road are in the hands of fate, with their lives at stake. Sometimes the planes fly low and aim their machine-guns at the stream of people below, killing men and animals. At such times the stream stops for a few minutes—but soon the movement continues, and even the terror of the moment is forgotten and is absorbed in the determined silence with which almost all these people bear their fate.

The entire population prefer to give up their homes rather than await Franco's Italian army. There was a constant stream of refugees from all classes of the population. And during all this time the Savoja, coming from Majorca, bombed the road.

Loyalist soldiers near Madrid, 1936

And the fine hope more often
than not ends like this.

Twenty-five years ago they posed for the photographs on that most hopeful day. And here is the credit balance. Into the future one dares not look.

Nowhere is there safety for anyone in this war. The women stay behind, but the death, the ingenious death from the skies finds them out.

There is little protection in the cities. The bombs break through the shelters. In Valencia, in Madrid, there is a daily toll.

Always the same: the sirens, the panic rush, the fracas of the bombs and then, as the dust settles, people go off to the morgue to wait, to see if by chance the son, the father, the mother who did not come home is on the list.

A little girl lies on a few bags. She's a pretty little girl, but she must be very tired, for she doesn't play with the other children. She hardly moves; only her big dark eyes follow all my movements. It's not easy always to stand aside and be unable to do anything except record the sufferings around one.

The defeated Loyalist Army of Spain crosses the border
into France led by a French policeman, 1939

For over six weeks, the civilian population and the Republican Army have been evacuated from Catalonia. About 400,000 people have crossed the border into France. This is perhaps the largest exodus in the history of humanity. Because of its special character, this exodus created new problems, for it concerned not only civilian refugees but also a whole army in retreat.

The first and largest of the Spanish refugee camps in France is at Argeles-sur-Mer. It is here that all the refugees were assembled at the beginning of the exodus. The camp is set up on an immense stretch of beach. Since that time, women, children, old men and some of the soldiers have been evacuated from it to other camps which are better equipped and more comfortable. And still today there are 50,000 men who live on the sand of Argeles-sur-Mer. Keeping up their morale after two and a half years of warfare and the terrible days of the exodus, these men manage to stand life in the camp, though in many ways it is harder for them to bear than the years of war.

The elite of a whole people live in these tents and shacks built on sand. Made almost unrecognizable by the gray sand, they have all begun to look alike. A glacial wind blows almost constantly and envelops the camp in a greyish cloud reminiscent of the nomad camps of Mongolia. The level of the campers' existence is hardly higher, as well as being deprived of their liberty. Scientists, musicians, peasants who have left the trenches for the first time in two and a half years mix freely with each other. One question is the same for all of them: what is to become of them?

China

In January 1938, Capa left Europe for the first time. He went on assignment to record a war on the other side of the world. In the fighting between the Chinese and the Japanese invaders of their country, he found mirrored the scenes he had left behind him in Spain.

Hankow, 1938

Hankow, 1938

Many peoples are represented in the huge Chinese nation. But all these peoples seem to be formed and bound together by something which so far has resisted even the heaviest storms of our times. One could get used to it and remember that almost every Chinese, even the most modern in his beliefs, has his roots in a time which is far removed from our bloody present. We Europeans also, who have invented all these arms and war machines, do not live only amidst the noise of battle.

I think I realized for the first time what is special about these people when I met the columns of the lightly wounded: slowly they marched by, single file, with bandages on their arms, their heads, their eyes, or their necks. Silent rows of men who had come from one of the heaviest battles in thousands of years of Chinese history. Surely many of them had seen terrible things, had passed horrible hours, days or weeks. But all terror had passed from their faces. Their fresh wounds must have hurt them—yet in their faces there was nothing of the tension with which European wounded fight to suppress their pain. They marched by calmly, almost indifferent to their own pain.

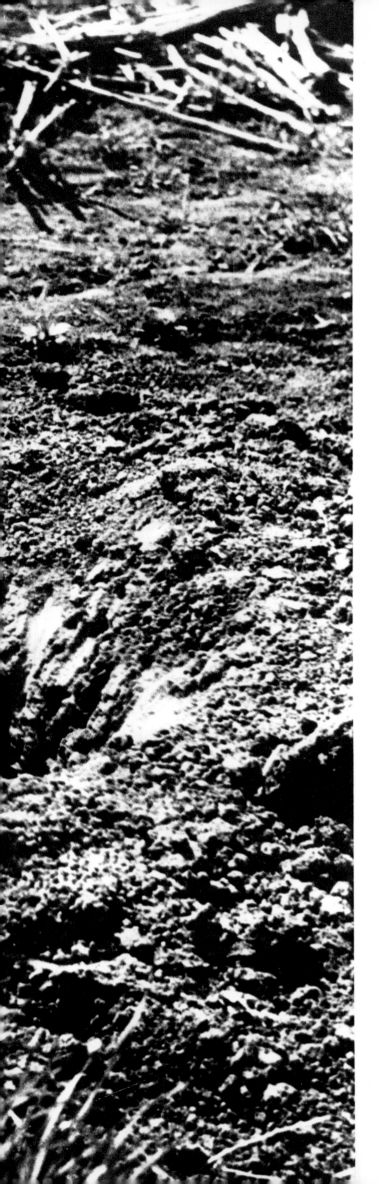

War is a task which one is irrevocably faced with; but it doesn't require any big illusion to cause a Chinese to give up his life. All this bears only remote resemblance to nationalism in the European sense of the word. The idea of nationalism which has begun to form in China during these last decades is at the same time less definite and more comprehensive than that of a European. Thus the Chinese will to stem the attack has an Asiatic depth and limitlessness.

Just think how much it may mean one day when this Chinese initiative will be used for tasks other than to resist the brunt of enemy attack.

WORLD WAR II

England

The last man to leave the plane was the pilot. He seemed to be all right except for a slight gash on his forehead. I moved to get a close-up. He stopped midway and cried, "Are these the pictures you were waiting for, photographer?" I shut my camera and left for London without saying goodbye.

On the train to London, with those successfully exposed rolls in my bag, I hated myself and my profession. This sort of photography was only for undertakers and I didn't like being one. If I was to share the funeral, I swore, I would have to share the procession.

Next morning, after sleeping it over, I felt better. While shaving I had a conversation with myself about the incompatibility of being a reporter and hanging onto a tender soul at the same time. The pictures of the guys sitting around the airfield without the pictures of their being hurt and killed would have given the wrong impression. The pictures of the dead and wounded were the ones that would show people the real aspect of war, and I was glad I had taken that one roll before I turned soppy.

English fighter pilot, 1941

St. John's Church, Waterloo, stands with its Grecian portico dominating the road. The clock has stopped at ten minutes to eleven. A little rubbish lying on the steps, an unnatural shaft of daylight shining out of the door instead of dark reverent shadows within, suddenly reveal that the church is a shell, its roof gone, and that the sun can pour in at will. A basket of geraniums is slung between the central columns. On the outside railings the vicar of the parish, Father Hutchinson, has placed a large notice written in black and red letters:

"In December this church was bombed. One hundred and fifty people in the crypt were unhurt. Give God the praise... The old church, mother of souls in this parish, true to her maternal instinct, gathered the full fury of the blow into her heart and gave her life for her children. Now we take to the crypt for our worship, as better Christians have done before us, until this church shall rise glorious from the ruins."

(Text from *The Battle of Waterloo Road*
by Diana Forbes-Robertson and Robert Capa.)

London, 1941

They are no braver than other people, in Lambeth, and no more terrified either. They have got through many nights of horror, and many lives have been lost, but in common with the whole of London it all does not really make any difference. Life continues in spite of the lights failing, the gas and water mains being hit. In spite of death, life in its ordinary regular drudging character is more durable than the desire to stop it. They find ways of getting through the bad times by laughing at them, by belittling them, by dramatizing them, by not understanding them.

Dear Mum,

　　Many thanks for your Christmas card which I received with Mrs. Field's on Monday last; it was a bit late, but very much appreciated. I also had a letter from Doris the same day; it was dated October 3rd, it shows how long we have to wait for a word from home. That particular letter and your cards took over four months.

　　Well, Mum, I am still keeping well; hope you are too and not suffering too much from the air raids . . .

　　I am really stuck as to what to say in letters nowadays; there is not very much news to tell you and I think I have told you in previous letters a little about the type of country I am in. You will also probably have read in the papers about this country (Eritrea) which I am in at the moment. The old army is doing some good work out here considering the strangeness of the country and the heat.

　　I must tell you about my cooking, Mum. I scrounged some flour, figs and baking powder, and mixed them all up for about two hours and believe me the result amazed me; it turned out a lovely fig roll, nearly as good as your boiled puddings . . . I tried my hand at a jam tart, but baking is not in my line. Had to make an oven out of petroleum tins and it was hard to keep a good fire going . . .

　　Has anything exciting happened in Waterloo since I have been away or is it continuing in its drab and weary way?

　　Give my love to Mrs. Field, and thank her for the card.

　　Cherio and look after yourself,

Lots of love,

Your son, John

North Africa

TIME magazine's Bill Lang and the GIs' Ernie Pyle, both oldtimers of the North African campaign, took me with them in their jeep. They promised to find me as much war as I needed for my health and my pictures. We headed for El Guetar, where the First Infantry Division was holding back the main German counter-attack.

We found plenty of war before we reached the front. German fighter planes were strafing the road and every few minutes we had to stop the jeep and jump into a ditch for cover. There was a lot of excitement, but I got no pictures at all.

Bill and Ernie stopped at Division headquarters. I was in a hurry to get my first pictures and they told me to go on ahead and cross two little jebels (what the Arabs call their hills) and hide between the jebels in the wadi (the Arab word for valley). "Just ask anybody where the war is," they said. "You can't miss it."

I found jebels and wadis. The 16th Infantry Regiment was dug in and the GIs were writing letters and reading pocket books in deep fox-holes. I asked them where the war was. They pointed to the next jebel. In every wadi, they pointed up to a jebel, and on every jebel they pointed down a wadi.

Finally, on the last and highest hilltop, I found about fifty soldiers relaxing and eating up cans of C-rations. Their faces were devoid of all enthusiasm. I walked up to their lieutenant and asked where all the shooting was. "It's hard to say," he answered. "My platoon has only the most advanced position on the front."

He consoled me with a can of C-rations. Just as I was about to dig into the awful-looking stew, a shell whistled and I threw myself flat on the ground, spilling the meat and beans all over me. It was a German shell all right, but it landed a few hundred yards away. When I raised my head the lieutenant—who hadn't budged—was looking down at me. He was very smug. Sheepishly I got up, dusted off the beans, and told him that from my angle this war was like an aging actress: more and more dangerous and less and less photogenic.

Late in the afternoon, the Germans withdrew, leaving behind twenty-four burned out tanks and a lot of very dead krauts.

I got all kinds of pictures: pictures of dust, pictures of smoke and of generals; but none of the tension and drama of battle which I could feel and follow with my naked eyes.

Our breakthrough to the sea and Tunis was bogged down, but we managed to stop the Germans from pushing us back and re-taking Gafsa. The First Division fought for three weeks on the jebels of El Guetar, and every day I took the same pictures of dust, smoke and death.

Italy

The Germans had pulled out during the night and had left the dead and wounded Italian civilians behind. We were lying around in the little square in front of the church, completely pooped and thoroughly disgusted. There wasn't much sense to this fighting, dying, taking pictures, I was thinking.

I didn't know any Italian, so in broken Spanish I tried to explain to the old man that only my great-grandfather was Sicilian. He answered with a stream of strange words. There was one word he kept repeating, "Brook-a-leen." One of my troopers caught on and pointed to himself. "Me, Brooklyn."

The conversation became easier and we established that Americans like Sicilians and Sicilians love Americans; that Americans don't like Germans and Sicilians hate Germans. These preliminaries over, I came to the point. Where were we, and were any Germans around?

The regiment was just jumping off to take Troina, a small town perched on a hilltop. Troina was tough. It took us seven days to capture it and we lost a lot of good men.

This was the first time I had followed an attack from beginning to end, and I managed to get some good pictures. They were simple pictures and showed how dreary and unspectacular fighting actually is. Scoops depend on luck and quick transmission, and most of them don't mean anything the day after they are published. But the soldier who looks at the shots of Troina, ten years from now in his home in Ohio, will be able to say, "That's how it was."

Troina, 1943

When headquarters found that there was no resistance in the town, they ordered us to stop and wait for the commanding general. We called headquarters unprintable names and waited. In a short while the corps commander arrived surrounded by aids and swarms of military police. The MPs promptly took over and blocked off any further advance by tanks, soldiers or war correspondents.

The general ordered the MPs to bring forward a few of the celebrating Italian gendarmes. The gendarmes were produced. The general said he didn't give a damn about their innocence; all he wanted was the Italian general in command of Palermo. The gendarmes nodded and said, "Yes, yes," but did not move. The exasperated general asked for an interpreter and I offered my services. I got the point over to the gendarmes somehow. I explained that the general wanted to avoid unnecessary bloodshed and wanted the Italian general to announce the terms of the surrender to the populace. The gendarmes nodded "Si, si," climbed into a jeep with a couple of MPs and took off toward the center of town.

In fifteen minutes the jeep reappeared. Seated in the back, between the two beaming gendarmes, was a very unhappy Italian major-general. The American general motioned the sweating Italian general into his command car and repeated his order to the MPs not to let anyone through. He had a white flag hoisted onto his car and it looked as if he was going to take Palermo without the Army.

Here goes my surrender ceremony, I thought. But just as the car was about to leave, the general turned toward me. "Interpreter, come along," he ordered.

We drove up to the governor's palace and dismounted in the courtyard. The American general demanded the immediate and unconditional surrender of the town and military district of Palermo. I translated it into French, the language I knew best, and hoped the Italian would understand me. He replied in perfect French that he would be only too glad to do so, but it was really impossible. He had already surrendered four hours earlier to an American infantry division that had entered the city from the opposite direction.

The American general became impatient at the delay. "Stop that jabbering, soldier! I want unconditional surrender and I want it immediately!"

I explained to the Italian that surrendering the second time ought to be much easier than the first. Besides, our general was the corps commander, and would undoubtedly allow him to keep his orderly and personal belongings in the prisoners' camp. The issue was won. He surrendered in French, Italian, and Sicilian, and asked whether he could keep his wife too.

My translator's job was done, and I went back to taking pictures. Later, when the surrender ceremony was over, I saw the Italian general being led away to prison—empty-handed and alone.

The road leading into the city was lined with
tens of thousands of frantic Sicilians waving white sheets and
homemade American flags with not enough stars and too many
stripes. Everyone had a cousin in Brook-a-leen.

Taking pictures of victory is like taking pictures of a
church wedding ten minutes after the departure of the
newlyweds. Some confetti still glittered among the filth of the
place, but the empty-stomached merrymakers had quickly
dispersed, already wondering how much the bride and groom
would quarrel the next day.

Palermo, 1943

Everyone hits the mud and stops dreaming about home, stops speculating about the if of our not being there, and the Germans maybe not being there. The hilltop is still two thousand yards away, and it is just as dangerous to stay as to go forward. So at every shell we hit the dirt, and then stand up and crouch forward until we hit the dirt again. Then someone yells for the first-aid men, and we are all sure that we will get it next.

I am on my stomach, my head behind a big stone, my flanks protected by two soldiers lying next to me. After every explosion I raise my head and take a picture of the flattened soldiers ahead of me, and of the thin, drifting smoke of the explosion. Overhead, the pattern of shells is approaching my hole, and I don't raise my head any more. A shell explodes ten yards away and something hits my behind. I am too scared to turn and look; the next one may hit even closer. Carefully, I feel my behind with my hand and find no blood, only a big rock which the exploding shell has thrown on me. The sergeant on my right gets a shrapnel which cuts his right arm just badly enough for a Purple Heart. The fellow on my left does not move at all, and will never get to open his Christmas package. Now the shells are falling away beyond us, and I light two cigarettes. The sergeant inhales deeply and hands me the first aid packet. I fix his arm. Looking at the wound, he says, "By New Year's I'll be back in the lines."

Late in the afternoon the fire subsides and the sergeant and I stand up and make a run for it. I have a dozen not unusual pictures, a big bruise on my behind, and my knees are wobbly. The Germans are still on the hilltop. I know it will be a long time before I want to go with any attack to take pictures again.

The rains started. The mud got deeper and deeper. Our shoes, designed for walking in garrison towns, thirstily drank in the water, and we slid two steps backward for each step forward. Our light shirts and trousers gave us no protection against the wind and rain. Our Army, the best equipped in the world, was stuck in those mountains, and it seemed we were not moving at all. With every costly five-hundred yard advance, Rome seemed farther and farther away.

I dragged myself from mountain to mountain, taking pictures of mud, misery and death.

In December I was climbing up the steep slopes of Mount Pantano. The 34th Infantry Division had been trying to reach the peak for the past ten or fifteen days, and had finally taken it the day before I arrived. The dead on the slopes were not yet buried. Every five yards a foxhole, in each at least one dead soldier. Around them, torn covers of pocket books soaked through and through, empty cans of C-rations, and faded bits of letters from home. The bodies of those who had dared to leave their holes were blocking my path. Their blood was dry and rusty, blending with the color of the late autumn leaves fallen about them.

The higher I climbed, the shorter the distances between the dead. I could not look any more. I stumbled on toward the hilltop, repeating to myself like an idiot, "I want to walk in the California sunshine and wear white shoes and white trousers."

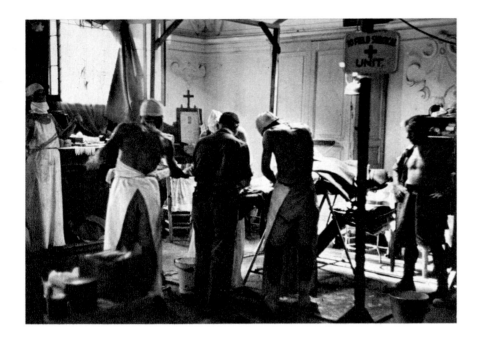

I found the hospital in a little church. It wasn't
hard to find: a long line of ambulances made a steady
procession toward it.

At the entrance to the church, the
ambulances were disgorging their blood-covered stretchers.
In the dark interior, the moaning of the wounded made
a strange kind of prayer, and the smell of ether blended
with that of incense. The church was full. Most of the
wounded had to lie on the cold floor. There were only
a few army cots, and they had been assigned to the
hopelessly wounded. Over their heads, like sacristy
lamps, hung plasma bottles, and the trickling blood tried
to catch their escaping lives.

Before the altar, kneeling alone, his back
to the congregation of wounded and dying, his face
pressed to the steps, was a soldier who seemed to be their
priest. He had no wounds that I could see, but a shell
had exploded near him and had shattered his nerves
and blown the senses out of his body. He mumbled a
steady stream of incoherent sounds, and only God knew
what he said.

Every morning we learned that during the night one of our best men had gone. We did not gamble, we did not drink, we did not shave. We did not file any stories, and, like the soldiers, waited only for that shell or for the spring.

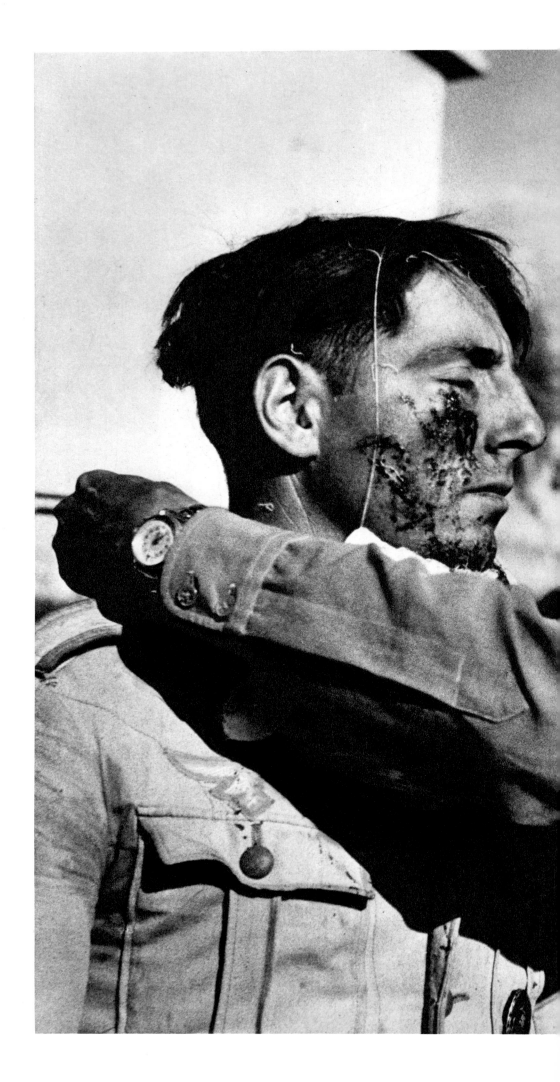

From November to Christmas the Fifth Army advanced less than ten miles, sank ten inches deeper in the mud. My underwear was stiff under the uniform I never took off. My pictures were sad and empty as the war, and I did not feel like sending them to the magazine.

In the lead was the Italian Army. They were afraid not only of the Americans, but of the Germans too, and ran in every direction. The Germans were slower than the Italians, but they retreated steadily. Behind us all, pushing us relentlessly forward, General Patton's tanks rumbled in the dust.

Naples

The narrow street leading to my hotel was blocked by a queue of silent people in front of a schoolhouse. It was not a food line because the people coming out of the building held only their hats in their hands. I fell in behind the queue. I entered the school and was met by the sweet, sickly smell of flowers and the dead. In the room were twenty primitive coffins, not well enough covered with flowers and too small to hide the dirty little feet of children—children old enough to fight the Germans and be killed, but just a little too old to fit in children's coffins.

These children of Naples had stolen rifles and bullets and had fought the Germans for fourteen days, while we had been pinned to the Chiunzi pass. These children's feet were my real welcome to Europe, I who had been born there. More real by far than the welcome of the hysterically cheering crowds I had met along the road, many of them the same that had yelled *"Duce!"* in an earlier year.

I took off my hat and got out my camera. I pointed the lens at the faces of the prostrated women, taking little pictures of their dead babies, until finally the coffins were carried away. Those were my truest pictures of victory, the ones I took at that simple schoolhouse funeral.

The Invasion

I would say that the war correspondent gets more drinks, more girls, better pay, and greater freedom than the soldier, but that at this stage of the game, having the freedom to choose his spot and being allowed to be a coward and not be executed for it is his torture. The war correspondent has his stake—his life—in his own hands, and he can put it on this horse or that horse, or he can put it back in his pocket at the very last minute.

I am a gambler. I decided to go in with Company E in the first wave.

June 6, 1944

Our pre-invasion breakfast was served at 3:00 a.m. The mess boys of the *U.S.S. Chase* wore immaculate white jackets and served hot cakes, sausages, eggs, and coffee with unusual zest and politeness. But the pre-invasion stomachs were preoccupied, and most of the noble effort was left on the plates.

At 4 a.m. we were assembled on the open deck. The invasion barges were swinging on the cranes, ready to be lowered. Waiting for the first ray of light, the two thousand men stood in perfect silence; whatever they were thinking, it was some kind of prayer.

I too stood very quietly. I was thinking a little bit of everything; of green fields, pink clouds, grazing sheep, all the good times, and very much of getting the best pictures of the day. None of us was at all impatient, and we wouldn't have minded standing in the darkness for a very long time. But the sun had no way of knowing that this day was different from all others, and rose on its usual schedule. The first-wavers stumbled into their barges, and—as if on slow-moving elevators—we descended into the sea. The sea was rough and we were wet before our barge pushed away from the mother ship. It was already clear that General Eisenhower would not lead his people across the Channel with dry feet or dry else.

In no time, the men started to puke. But this was a polite as well as a carefully prepared invasion, and little paper bags had been provided for the purpose. Soon the puking hit a new low. I had an idea this would develop into the father and mother of all D-days.

The coast of Normandy was still miles away when the first unmistakable popping reached our listening ears. We ducked down in the puky water in the bottom of the barge and ceased to watch the approaching coast line. The first empty barge, which had already unloaded its troops on the beach, passed us on the way back to the *Chase* and the Negro boatswain gave us a happy grin and the V sign. It was now light enough to start taking pictures, and I brought my first Contax camera out of its waterproof oilskin. The flat bottom of our barge hit the earth of France. The boatswain lowered the steel-covered barge front, and there, between the grotesque designs of steel obstacles sticking out of the water, was a thin line of sand covered with smoke—our Europe, the "Easy Red" beach.

My beautiful France looked sordid and uninviting, and a German machine gun, spitting bullets around the barge, fully spoiled my return. The men from my barge waded in the water. Waist-deep, with rifles ready to shoot, with the invasion obstacles and the smoking beach in the background—this was good enough for the photographer. I paused for a moment on the gangplank to take my first real picture of the invasion. The boatswain who was in an understandable hurry to get the hell out of there, mistook my picture-taking attitude for explicable hesitation, and helped me make up my mind with a well-aimed kick in the rear. The water was cold and the beach still more than a hundred yards away. The bullets tore holes in the water around me, and I made for the nearest steel obstacle. A soldier got there at the same time, and for a few minutes we shared its cover. He took the waterproofing off his rifle, and began to shoot without much aiming at the smoke-ridden beach. The sound of his rifle gave him enough courage to move forward and he left the obstacle to me. It was a foot larger now, and I felt safe enough to take pictures of the other guys hiding just like I was.

It was still very early and very gray for good pictures, but the gray water and the gray sky made the little men, dodging under the surrealistic designs of Hitler's anti-invasion brain trust, very effective.

I finished my pictures, and the sea was cold in my trousers. Reluctantly, I tried to move away from my steel pole, but the bullets chased me back every time. Fifty yards ahead of me, one of our half-burnt amphibious tanks stuck out of the water and offered me my next cover. I sized up the situation. There was little future for the elegant raincoat heavy on my arm. I dropped it and made for the tank. Between floating bodies I reached it, paused for a few more pictures, and gathered my guts for the last jump to the beach.

Now the Germans played on all their instruments and I could not find any hole between the shells and bullets that blocked the last twenty-five yards to the beach. I just stayed behind my tank, repeating a little sentence from my Spanish Civil war days, *"Es una cosa muy seria. Es una cosa muy seria."*—This is a very serious business.

The tide was coming in, and now the water reached the farewell letter to my family in my breast pocket. Behind the human cover of the last two guys, I reached the beach. I threw myself flat and my lips touched the earth of France. I had no desire to kiss it.

Jerry still had plenty of ammunition left, and I fervently wished I could be beneath the earth now and above later. The chances to the contrary were becoming increasingly strong. I turned my head sideways and found myself nose to nose with a lieutenant from our last night's poker game. He asked me if I knew what he saw. I told him no and that I didn't think he could see much beyond my head. "I'll tell you what I see," he whispered, "I see my ma on the front porch, waving my insurance policy."

St. Laurent-sur-Mer must have been at one time a drab, cheap resort for vacationing French schoolteachers. Now, on June 6, 1944, it was the ugliest beach in the whole world. Exhausted from the water and the fear, we lay flat on a small strip of wet sand between the sea and the barbed wire. The slant of the beach gave us some protection, so long as we lay flat, from the machine gun and rifle bullets, but the tide pushed us against the barbed wire, where the guns were enjoying open season. I crawled on my stomach over to my friend Larry, the Irish padre of the regiment, who could swear better than any amateur. He growled at me, "You damn half-Frenchy! If you don't like it here, why the hell did you come back?" Thus comforted by religion, I took out my second Contax camera and began to shoot without raising my head.

From the air "Easy Red" must have looked like an open tin of sardines. Shooting from the sardine's angle, the foreground of my pictures was filled with wet boots and green faces. Above the boots and faces, my picture frames were filled with shrapnel smoke; burnt tanks and sinking barges formed my background. Larry had a dry cigarette. I reached in my hip pocket for my silver flask and offered it to him. He tilted his head sideways and took a swig from the corner of his mouth. Before returning the bottle he gave it to my other chum, the Jewish medic, who very successfully imitated Larry's technique. The corner of my mouth was good enough for me too.

The next mortar shell fell between the barbed wire and the sea, and every piece of shrapnel found a man's body. The Irish priest and the Jewish doctor were the first to stand up on the "Easy Red" beach. I shot the picture. The next shell fell even closer. I didn't dare to take my eyes off the finder of my Contax and frantically shot frame after frame. Half a minute later, my camera jammed—my roll was finished. I reached in my bag for a new roll, and my wet, shaking hands ruined the roll before I could insert it in the camera.

I paused for a moment ... and then I had it bad.

The empty camera trembled in my hands. It was a new kind of fear shaking my body from toe to hair, and twisting my face. I unhooked my shovel and tried to dig a hole. The shovel hit stone under the sand and I hurled it away. The men around me lay motionless. Only the dead on the water line rolled with waves. An LCI braved the fire, and medics with red crosses painted on their helmets poured from it. I did not think and I didn't decide it. I just stood up and ran toward the boat. I stepped into the sea between two bodies and the water reached to my neck. The rip tide hit my body and every wave slapped my face under my helmet. I held my cameras high above my head, and suddenly I knew that I was running away. I tried to turn but couldn't face the beach, and told myself, "I am just going to dry my hands on that boat."

I reached the boat. The last medics were just getting out. I climbed aboard. As I reached the deck I felt a shock, and suddenly was all covered with feathers. I thought, "What is this? Is somebody killing chickens?" Then I saw that the superstructure had been shot away and that the feathers were the stuffing from the kapok jackets of the men that had been blown up. The skipper was crying. His assistant had been blown up all over him, and he was a mess.

Our boat was listing and we slowly pulled away from the beach to try and reach the mother ship before we sank. I went down to the engine room, dried my hands and put fresh films in both cameras. I got back up on deck again in time to take one last picture of the smoke-covered beach. Then I took some shots of the crew giving transfusions on the open deck. An invasion barge came alongside and took us off the sinking boat. The transfer of the badly wounded on the heavy seas was a difficult business. I took no more pictures. I was busy lifting stretchers. The barge brought us to the *U.S.S. Chase,* the very boat I had left only six hours before. On the *Chase,* the last wave of the 16th Infantry was just being lowered, but the decks were already full with returning wounded and dead.

This was my last chance to return to the beach. I did not go. The mess boys who had served our coffee in white jackets and with white gloves at three in the morning were covered with blood and were sewing the dead in white sacks.

Seven days later, I learned that the pictures I had taken on "Easy Red" were the best of the invasion. But the excited darkroom assistant, while drying the negatives, had turned on too much heat and the emulsions had melted and run down before the eyes of the London office. Out of one hundred and six pictures in all, only eight were salvaged.

France

I joined Patton's fast-moving Fourth Armored Division as it drove toward Brittany along the coastal road. On both sides of the road, the happy French were shouting, *"Bonne chance!"* And the happy signposts read, "90 kilometers . . . 80 kilometers . . . to Paris."

The little coastal town of Brehal was the first town we reached that was unscarred by war. The Germans were on the run, and the good campaign began. Here the French were full happy. The food was good, and the first glass of wine was free in the bars.

The Germans were tough in their well-prepared fortress, but not so tough that they fought to the last German—only to the first American that got close enough to be dangerous. Then they threw up their hands, shouted *"Kamerad!"* and asked for cigarettes.

The sun was in a hurry to rise that morning, and we did not bother to brush our teeth.

The road to Paris was open, and every Parisian was out in the street to touch the first tank, to kiss the first man, to sing and cry. Never were there so many who were so happy so early in the morning.

I felt that this entry into Paris had been made especially for me. On a tank made by the Americans who had accepted me, riding with the Spanish Republicans with whom I had fought against Fascism long years ago, I was returning to Paris—the beautiful city where I first learned to eat, drink, and love.

The thousands of faces in the finder of my camera became more and more blurred; that finder was very, very wet. We drove through the *quartier* where I had lived for six years, passed my house by the lion of Belfort. My concierge was waving a handkerchief, and I was yelling to her from the rolling tank, *"C'est moi, c'est moi!"*

Around the Chamber of Deputies we had to fight, and some of the lipstick got washed off with blood. Late in the evening, Paris was free.

The people of Paris had
arisen and were fighting the Germans
in the streets by themselves.

South of St. Lo, 1944

Newly captured German officers being marched to prison camp,
followed by a French tart, who wished to stay with her customers.
St. Malo, 1944

The liberation of Paris
was the most unforgettable
day in the world.

Collaborator,
Chartres, 1944

Germany

The beginning of the end, the great airborne invasion of Germany started out in French boxcars dating from the First World War and bearing the well-known inscription "40 *hommes et 8 chevaux.*" The U.S. 17th Airborne Division was packed in long freight trains, and for forty-eight hours we were shuffled all over France. This was to deceive the enemy spies. After two days of this hocus-pocus, our generals decided that both the troops and the German spies were quite tired enough, and we arrived at an enclosed camp next to an airfield, sixty miles from the spot from which we started.

At the camp, we had a short time left for the usual pre-invasion cleaning of rifles and consciences. The day before the jump we were briefed and told that we would be jumping, together with an English airborne division, on the other side of the Rhine, right in the heart of the main German defense line.

Parachute jump on the Rhine, 1945

I flew in the lead plane with the regimental commander, and I was to be number two man in the jump right behind him. Before boarding the plane, the G-2 major had taken me aside. If anything happened to the Old Man when we got the signal to jump, I was instructed to boot him through the door. It was a very important and comforting feeling.

Our planes flew low over France. Through the open door of the plane the boys watched the landscape of a now peaceful France pass quickly by. Nobody puked; this was a very different invasion.

Thousands of planes and gliders had taken off simultaneously from fields in England and France, and we rendezvoused over Belgium. From there we flew on together in tight formation. Our shadows travelled on the roads and streets of the liberated countries, and we could see the faces of people waving to us. Even the dogs were fascinated and ran after our shadows. On both sides of us were planes towing gliders, and it looked as if someone had spun strings from the Channel to the Rhine, and then had hung from them, at intervals of a hundred yards, a lot of toy airplanes.

I put on an act and began to read a mystery story. At 10:15 I was only up to page sixty-seven, and the red light came on to get ready. For a moment I had the foolish idea of saying, "Sorry, I cannot jump. I have to finish my story."

I stood up, made sure that my cameras were well strapped to my legs and that my flask was in my breast pocket over my heart.

We still had fifteen minutes before the jump. I started to think over my whole life. It was like a movie where the projection machine has gone crazy, and I saw and felt everything I ever ate, ever did, and got to the end of it in twelve minutes flat. I felt very empty, and still had three minutes to go. I was standing in the open door behind the colonel. Six hundred feet below us was the Rhine. Then bullets began to hit our plane like pebbles. The green light flashed and I did not have to kick the colonel. The boys yelled "Umbriago!" I counted one thousand, two thousand, three thousand, and up above me was the lovely sight of my open parachute. The forty seconds to earth were hours on my grandfather clock, and I had plenty of time to unstrap my camera, take a few pictures and think of six or seven different things before I hit the ground. On the ground I kept clicking my shutter. We lay flat on the ground and nobody wanted to get up. The first fear was over, and we were reluctant to begin the second.

Ten yards away were tall trees, and some of the men who had jumped after me had landed in them and now were hanging helplessly fifty feet from the good earth.

A German machine-gun opened up at the dangling men. I began a long, loud Hungarian swear, and buried my head in the grass. A boy lying near me looked up.

"Stop those Jewish prayers," he called, "They won't help you now."

At 11 a.m. I had two rolls of film taken and I lit a cigarette. At 11:30 I took the first swig from my flask. We were firmly established on the other side of the Rhine. Our regiment had gotten the guns out of the wrecked gliders and we reached the road we were supposed to occupy and hold. We lost many of our men, but this was easier than Salerno or Anzio or Normandy. The Germans of those campaigns could have murdered us here, but these Germans were beaten.

Retracing the road our Army had travelled was like visiting a movie set two weeks after the picture was finished—some of the props were still lying around.

147

We reached a bridge leading into town. The first platoons were already crossing it, and we were very afraid it was going to be blown up any minute. A fashionable apartment building stood on the corner overlooking the bridge, and I climbed up to the fourth floor to see if the last picture of crouching and advancing infantry men could be the last picture of the war for my camera. Putting up a machine gun to cover the advance, a sergeant and one of his men moved out onto the open, unprotected balcony. I watched them from the door. When the gun had been set up, the sergeant returned. The young corporal pulled the trigger and began to shoot.

The last man shooting the last gun was not much different from the first. By the time the picture got to New York, no one would want to publish the picture of a simple soldier shooting an ordinary gun. But the boy had a clean, open, very young face, and his gun was still killing Fascists. I clicked my shutter, my first picture in weeks—and the last one of the boy alive.

Silently, the tense body of the gunner relaxed, and he slumped and fell back into the apartment. His face was not changed except for a tiny hole between his eyes. The puddle of blood grew beside his fallen head, and his pulse had long stopped beating.

I had the picture of the last man to die. The last day, some of the best ones die. But those alive will fast forget.

Jewish New Year services were held for the few survivors of the Jewish population of Berlin in one of the very few synagogues which escaped destruction. It had been rebuilt with the help of the U.S. Army.

Most of the Jews present were the only survivors of their families: children without parents, fathers without wives and women who lost their men and children. They were praying and singing, and many broke into tears when the Rabbi reminded them of the gas chambers where their families were exterminated.

The Berlin Jews did not have much to look forward to in the New Year and were resigned to their fate, being the last survivors without a future.

Berlin, 1945

During the Spanish civil conflict I
became a war photographer. Later I
photographed the "phony war" and
ended up taking pictures of the hot war.
When all this was over I was very
happy to become an unemployed war
photographer, and I hope to stay
unemployed as a war photographer till
the end of my life.

Warsaw, 1948

Israel

When World War II was over, Robert Capa could not remain unemployed as a war photographer. In 1948 he was on the central front in Israel, taking the first front-line pictures to come out of that embattled country. His photographs were of the Jewish settlements (Kibbutzim) scattered among the Arab villages—Kibbutzim under constant fire from the ground and bombing from the air. They were being defended by an army of born Palestinians mingled with immigrants from European concentration camps. And Capa was there, recording it all.

These men are on the road to Jerusalem. None of them ever got there. Many of them died on the other side of the ridge. Some are natives of the land on which they are fighting, but the majority were born in Budapest and Vienna and other cities and villages of Central Europe. A few days before the picture was taken, they were hustled off the immigrant boats at Haifa harbor, sketchily armed and trained, packed into the buses of Tel Aviv, and sent to lift the siege of Jerusalem. This they never did. They were stopped at Latrun by the Arab Legion in the bloodiest engagement of the war. But to meet their attacks, the Legion had to pull away many of their troops from Jerusalem, and the defenders there, with the pressure against them lessened, managed to save half the city.

This story is a fair resume of the condition of the state of Israel. The improvised means, the unready men, the sacrifice not quite altogether in vain, the half-won city, the plans that did not quite work out, the result not what was hoped for but not disastrous, history going in a slightly different direction from what had been expected—all this combines to produce a state which the early Zionists never imagined but in which a million Jews have found sanctuary from their enemies and can wrestle with their own destiny.

(Text from
Report on Israel
by Irwin Shaw
and Robert Capa.)

Immigration camp,
Israel, 1948

158

Every morning two or three boats carrying about 1,000 passengers enter the bay of Haifa harbor. The modern buildings of the new city gleam in the brilliant sunshine, and a thousand pairs of hungry eyes stare at them from the docks. The year-old state of Israel now has a Jewish population of 900,000 and receives a thousand more every day. Which means that in its first year, the new state absorbed half as much again as its original population.

The immigrants on these boat decks are the motley remains of a people who two thousand years ago left these shores to scatter to the far corners of the earth and are now coming back, most of them to live and some to die in the Holy Land.

The people on the deck are no longer hysterical, desperate, weeping, struggling immigrants, but a subdued people who gather in small groups on deck, exchanging the past and guessing about the future.

Every third arm on this boat has a blue number tattooed on it, and every bearer of a blue number has been through scores of concentration camps and D.P. camps from Eastern Poland through Germany and down to the Italian coast where they finally boarded the Theodore Herzl for Israel. The escapees of the barbed-wire form close groups in the middle of the boat deck and the other immigrants keep apart from them.

Among all these people, at most only one-third are really fitted for the hard work and tough conditions of the struggling new state. But the doors of Israel are open to any and every Jew who wants to enter, and the Jewish state of less than a million, surrounded by millions of Arabs, desperately needs their numbers.

Curiously, the present state owes its existence just as much to Hitler and Bevin as to its own accomplishments. Without Nazism it could never have gotten mass immigration and without Bevin to encourage the Arabs to fight and flee, it would never have gotten its present territory. But the new country, born out of victorious battle, is granted no peace.

Dr. Weizmann's eyes are failing. He spends most of his afternoons peacefully meditating in his cool garden with his little grandson for company. The trials and errors of Zionism lie behind him, and the trials and errors of the new state must be carried by the younger generation.

Dr. Weizmann, nearly blind president of the newly created state of Israel, casts his ballot at the first election. 1948.

The faith and future of all these conflicting people and ideals rest on the shoulders of a score of early immigrants from western Russia who head the first government of Israel. The problems they face now are graver than a year ago when five Arab armies were converging upon the little country. They must settle the hundreds of thousands of new immigrants, and to do this must create new industries and increase exports. They must keep a balance between the conflicting ideologies which were born in the orthodox ghettos of Warsaw, in the Bolshevist underground of prerevolutionary Russia, in the business districts of the East Sides of London and New York, and behind the bars of British jails under the Palestine mandate.

These men have worked sixteen hours a day for the last thirty years towards the realization of their dream, and their working day is no shorter now that they have become the first ministers of the government of Israel.

But the land is alive. In this country where nearly every village and town has a Biblical name and a legend attached to it, during the recent years of fighting the old names have acquired new legends for the future citizens. From north to south, every settlement had its own battle, created its own heroes.

Indo-China

HANOI, MAY 25, 1954

HE SAID: "THIS IS GOING TO BE A BEAUTIFUL STORY"

by JOHN MECKLIN

(TIME–LIFE correspondent who was with Capa on his last mission)

In the bug-ridden room of a Nam Dinh establishment which calls itself the Modern Hotel (in English), Bob Capa sucked a glass of warm cognac and soda and made a pronouncement: "This is maybe the last good war. The trouble with all you guys who complain so much about French public relations is that you don't appreciate this is a reporter's war. Nobody knows anything and nobody tells you anything, and that means a good reporter is free to go out and get a beat every day."

Capa and I had been touring French outposts in the besieged Red River Delta with General Rene Cogny, French commander in northern Vietnam. Next day we were going out with a 2,000-man task force which was to relieve, then evacuate, two garrisons some 50 miles south of Hanoi. Capa prepared for the mission with professional finesse: a thermos of iced tea, a jug of cognac, a jeep promoted from a French colonel, everything except matches. Capa never had matches, presumably because other people could be counted on for such obvious items.

When the jeep appeared at 7 a.m. May 25 we climbed in along with Scripps-Howard Correspondent Jim Lucas. Waiting for the Red River ferry just outside Nam Dinh, Capa announced, "This is going to be a beautiful story. I shall be on my good behavior today. I shall not insult people and I shall not even mention the excellence of my work."

On his delta tour Capa had got the idea of a picture story to be entitled "Bitter Rice." His plan was to dramatize the contrast of tanks next to peasants working in paddies, of men dying in the struggle for the rice harvest. All morning he worked to photograph peasants carrying rice to market in straw baskets, plodding along the edges of vehicle-clogged roads. Once a French motorcyclist playfully rode close to the roadside as he passed lines of peasants, forcing them to jump off. Said Capa, "Look at that s.o.b. making new Vietminh." When the column was stopped by ambushes, mines and trenches across the road, Capa was everywhere but always showing an expertness in calculated risk that only a man in his fifth war could know. He was cautious about crossing exposed areas, but if he saw a good picture which could only be made with risk he took the risk. A colonel invited us to lunch at Dong Qui Thon, but Capa kept poking around for pictures and failed to show up. We found him dozing under a truck and asked how his film was holding out. Said Capa, "That's what I'm doing here, saving film."

A few minutes later we heard that French Union elements had reached Doai Than, the first of two posts the column was to relieve. We got there in about 10 minutes, arriving at 2:25 p.m. Capa wanted to press on, saying: "The story's almost done, but I need the fort blowing up."

A couple of hundred yards beyond Doai Than the column was stalled again by a Vietminh ambush. We turned into the field and talked to the sector commander, Lieut. Colonel Jean Lacapelle. Capa asked, "What's new?"

The colonel's reply was a familiar one: "*Viets partout*" ("Vietminh everywhere"). As the column began moving again Capa climbed on the jeep hood for a shot. A truck loaded with infantry behind us tooted vigorously but Capa took his time. "That was a good picture," he said as he climbed down. But the column halted again almost immediately. This was at a point one kilometer past Doai Than and three kilometers short of the final objective, Thanh Ne. The road was three or four feet above the paddies and here served as a dike for a little stream which ran along the right side. About 50 yards ahead the road bent to the left, forming a V with the stream, now contained by an independent dike.

The sun beat down fiercely. There was firing in every direction: French artillery, tanks and mortars behind us, the chatter of small arms from woods surrounding a village 500 yards to our left, heavy small-arms fire mixed with exploding French shells in another village 500 yards ahead and to our right, the sporadic ping of slugs passing overhead, the harrowing *curr-rump* of mines and enemy mortars.

A young Vietnamese lieutenant approached us and began practicing his English, which was limited to a labored "How are you sir? I am good." Capa was exquisitely bored and climbed up on the road, saying, "I'm going up the road a little bit. Look for me when you get started again." This was about 2:50 p.m. The lieutenant switched to French and asked if we liked Vietnam.

At 2:55 the earth shook from a heavy explosion. Behind us spouted up a column of brown smoke and flames: the French were blowing up Doai Than. Asked the lieutenant, "Does the atomic bomb look like that?" Said Lucas, "Dammit, there goes the picture Capa wanted."

A few minutes later a tank began firing right behind us. The French were mortaring the village to our left and at 3:05 Moroccan infantrymen began advancing through the paddies to finish the job. I was making notes on this when a helmeted soldier arrived and spoke to the lieutenant in Vietnamese.

Without a trace of emotion the lieutenant said, "*Le photographe est mort*" ("The photographer is dead"). I understood the words but they didn't register and I said, "Pardon?" The lieutenant repeated the sentence in the same flat voice. This time the words registered, but I was certain I had misunderstood and said to Lucas almost as a joke, "This guy's trying to tell me Capa's dead."

Still deadpan, the lieutenant spelled out the English word with French pronunciation of the letters: *day euh aah tay aash* (death). Simultaneously a second Vietnamese ran up and beckoned directly to me. The lieutenant questioned him and relayed, "Maybe not dead but wounded by mortar, *tres grave*" ("very serious").

Lucas and I jumped up and ran with the soldier down the ditch. At the point where the road bent soldiers pointed up and over the road, then disappeared. We scrambled across the road and into a small lowland field. At the foot of the dike across the V formed by the bending road Capa lay on his back, the stump of his shattered left leg about a foot from a hole blown in the earth by the explosion. He also had a grievous chest wound. One camera was clutched in his left hand. I began calling his name. The second or third time his lips moved slightly like those of a man disturbed in sleep. That was his last movement. It was 3:10 p.m.

I called to a Moroccan soldier to get a medic. The medic, a husky Frenchman with a stretcher, took one look, shrugged and started to go. Then he turned and asked, "*Camarade?*" When I nodded he shrugged again and opened the stretcher. Still thinking Capa had been hit by a mortar, we hurried to a less exposed spot across the road.

An instant later there was a thunderous explosion on the road above us. The blast blew screaming Vietnamese soldiers, miraculously uninjured, into the ditch. A bulldozer had set off a mine, and less than a minute later another went off. Investigation revealed they were all anti-personnel mines, and it is almost certain that Capa stepped on one of these.

The exploding mines brought Colonel Lacapelle charging forward. He flagged an ambulance and hurried Capa back to Dong Qui Thon, five kilometers away. There a Vietnamese doctor pronounced him dead. Said the operation commander, Lieut. Colonel Jacques Navarre, General Henri Navarre's brother, "*C'est l'Indochine, monsieur*" ("This is Indochina"). Then he turned and walked away past the truck where Capa had lain dozing less than two hours before.

The doctor asked, "Is this the first American correspondent killed in Indochina?" I said yes. He said, "It is a harsh way for America to learn."

At Nam Dinh, where the casket was loaded aboard a C-47 for shipment to Hanoi, Zone Commander Colonel Paul Vanuxen turned out a Senegalese honor guard. In Saigon General Navarre sent condolences to the U.S. embassy. In Hanoi, where the body was taken to the French cemetery for temporary burial, General Cogny ordered an honor guard of 19 red-bereted colonial paratroopers and sent a large wreath. There was also a wreath from the army's press information service and a third wreath inscribed "*A notre ami.*" It was from *La Bonne Casserole*, a local restaurant where Capa terrified the waiters, charmed the hostess and taught the bartender to mix American martinis.

At the cemetery General Cogny, in dress uniform, stood at salute for a minute before the casket, turned to newsmen and delivered a brief emotional speech. Capa, he said, "fell as a soldier among soldiers." Then he pinned a medal on the American flag draped over the casket. It was one of France's highest honors: Croix de Guerre with Palm, Order of the Army.